U. S. CHEMICAL SAFETY AND HAZARD INVESTIGATION BOARD

# INVESTIGATION REPORT

## STEEL MANUFACTURING INCIDENT

(2 Killed, 4 Injured)

**BETHLEHEM STEEL CORPORATION**
BURNS HARBOR DIVISION
CHESTERTON, INDIANA
FEBRUARY 2, 2001

**KEY ISSUES:**

- MAINTENANCE JOB PLANNING
- FACILITY WINTERIZATION AND DEADLEGS
- LINE AND EQUIPMENT OPENING
- DECOMMISSIONING AND DEMOLITION

REPORT NO. 2001-02-I-IN

ISSUE DATE: JANUARY 2002

# CONTENTS

# FIGURES

3

# ACRONYMS AND ABBREVIATIONS

AFL-CIO            American Federation of Labor and Congress of Industrial Organizations

CFR                 Code of Federal Regulations

COG                Coke oven gas

CSB                U.S. Chemical Safety and Hazard Investigation Board

°F                  Degrees Fahrenheit

$ft^3$/day            Cubic feet per day

IOSHA            Indiana Occupational Safety and Health Administration

MSDS            Material Safety Data Sheet

OSHA            Occupational Safety and Health Administration

# EXECUTIVE SUMMARY

## ES. 1  Introduction

On February 2, 2001, a fire occurred at Bethlehem Steel Corporation's Burns Harbor mill in Chesterton, Indiana. One Bethlehem Steel millwright and one contractor supervisor died. Four Bethlehem Steel millwrights were injured, one seriously. Workers were attempting to remove a slip blind[1] and a cracked valve from a coke oven gas (COG) line leading to a decommissioned furnace. During removal of the valve, flammable liquid was released and ignited.

Because of the serious nature of the incident, the U.S. Chemical Safety and Hazard Investigation Board (CSB) launched an investigation to determine the root and contributing causes and to issue recommendations to help prevent similar occurrences.

## ES. 2  Incident

In 1992, the #4 batch furnace in the 160-inch plate mill was decommissioned, which created a deadleg[2] in the COG piping. The furnace had been undergoing demolition since summer 2000.

On January 1, 2001, coke oven gas was found to be leaking from a crack in a 10-inch valve used to close off the COG line that fed the out-of-service #4 furnace. The crack was likely caused by the freezing and expansion of water in COG condensate that had accumulated above the valve.

Coke oven gas is a byproduct of the cokemaking process in an integrated steel mill. It is used throughout the mill as a gaseous fuel. At the point of distribution, coke oven gas typically contains up to 10 percent water vapor. As it passes through cold distribution

---

[1] A slip blind (referred to as a pancake blind at Burns Harbor) is a round metal plate that is slipped between the loosened flanges of a piping connection to prevent flow.
[2] A deadleg is a section of piping, typically vertical, without flow. In this case, it was connected to the main COG piping.

lines, a portion of the water and heavier hydrocarbons[3] condense out of the gas. These liquids drain into tanks at various locations along the COG distribution system.

On January 5, millwrights installed a slip blind in the piping at the upper flange of the cracked valve to stop the leak. This allowed liquid to again collect in the deadleg, which lacked a low point drain.

Upstream of the #4 furnace, pipe insulation was missing from condensate drain lines on the roof of the plate mill. The missing insulation–combined with freezing temperatures in December 2000 and January 2001–caused the drain lines to plug with ice, which prevented the removal of condensate from the COG piping. It is most likely that flammable liquid concentrated and accumulated in the deadleg as the water trapped in the piping froze. The inability to remove condensate also resulted in three incidents prior to February 2–including one on January 30, in which a large surge of fire and burning liquid were emitted from another furnace.

On Friday, February 2, millwrights were assigned to replace the blind and cracked valve with a blind flange and drain assembly. A vacuum truck crew from Onyx Industrial Services was assigned to remove the condensate, which was expected to be non-flammable.

There was no way to safely drain the deadleg prior to opening the flange. As the millwrights loosened and removed the bolts from around the blind, a small stream of liquid began to seep from the flange. The valve and the slip blind suddenly dropped down several inches against the loosened bolts. Flammable condensate sprayed out and soaked two of the millwrights and the Onyx supervisor. The condensate ignited. CSB identified an infrared heat lamp and a natural gas-fired space heater–both used for freeze protection–as two potential ignition sources. As the flame reached the valve and the now open pipe, there was a blast and flammable liquid sprayed in all directions.

---

[3] The heavier hydrocarbons include benzene, toluene, and xylenes.

The two millwrights were engulfed in flames and fell behind the furnace structure. One of these millwrights died; the other suffered burns and contusions. The Onyx supervisor fell onto the demolition debris and was fatally burned. In escaping through the flames, a third millwright received serious burns and another suffered smoke inhalation.

## ES. 3   Key Findings

1.  The #4 batch furnace was decommissioned in 1992, which created a deadleg of 25 feet of vertical 10-inch-diameter piping where COG condensate collected. The foreseeable sequence of events `that could lead to the accumulation and freezing of water in the deadleg was not taken into account in planning the decommissioning work.

2.  Missing pipe insulation caused water in the COG condensate to freeze and plug the system drains at the 160-inch plate mill in December 2000. It is most likely that the condensate trapped in the COG piping separated into water and hydrocarbon layers. As the water layer continued to freeze, liquid hydrocarbons accumulated in the COG piping and were carried into the furnace piping.

3.  Three incidents in the 160-inch plate mill in January 2001, including one that produced a surge of fire and a flow of flaming liquid from a furnace, demonstrated that the amount of condensate in the COG system was unusually high and could be flammable. The Burns Harbor facility did not have a system for monitoring and controlling hazards that could be caused by changes in COG condensate accumulation rates or flammability. Burns Harbor staff was investigating these incidents and conducting followup activities at the time of the February 2 incident. Knowledge of the previous incidents was not shared with the workforce performing the maintenance job on February 2.

4.  The majority of the Burns Harbor and contractor personnel interviewed by CSB considered COG condensate to be mostly water; they did not think that it posed a fire risk. The potential presence of flammables was not considered in job

planning. The Material Safety Data Sheet (MSDS) for COG condensate does not list the potential for flammability. A sample of COG condensate taken by CSB from another furnace in the plate mill after February 2 was highly flammable, with a flash point of 29 degrees Fahrenheit (°F).[4]

5. The installation of the slip blind above the cracked valve on January 5 and the attempted removal of the leaking valve on February 2 were both done without written procedures, as required by the Burns Harbor Lockout, Blue Flag, and Tag policy and the Burns Harbor Gas Hazard Control Program. These procedures required detailed written instructions for isolation, drainage, and purging of piping.

6. The initial leak repair plan was to install a blind flange and drain valve to replace the cracked valve. However, a slip blind was installed to save time. The slip blind created a hazardous situation; it allowed COG condensate to again accumulate in the deadleg and prevented safe draining of the line because there was no low point drain.

7. The demolition work at the #4 furnace was being conducted without sufficient planning, oversight, or control. Demolition activities resulted in elevated walkways without railings and obstructed egress pathways, which prevented workers from quickly escaping when the ignition occurred.

## ES. 4  Root Causes

1. **Management systems for the supervision, planning, and execution of maintenance work were inadequate.**

   - Burns Harbor mill personnel often bypassed the Lockout, Blue Flag, and Tag and Gas Hazard Control Program procedures when performing COG line maintenance in the steel handling areas of the facility. Company requirements for written

---

[4] Flash point is the minimum temperature at which a liquid gives off sufficient vapor to form an ignitable mixture with air near the surface. Liquids with flash points of less than 100°F are classified as flammable.

planning, job setup, and line isolation and purging were not followed on January 5 or February 2.

- The work on January 5 and February 2 should not have been scheduled without a plan to control the hazards created by the potential for flammables and by the lack of a low point drain in the deadleg.

- Personnel performing the work were not made aware of the possible presence of flammables, nor were they informed of the condensate incidents that occurred prior to February 2.

- Obstructed exit routes due to demolition work on the #4 furnace were not considered during job planning.

- Insulation was not reinstalled after the completion of maintenance work on an outdoor section of system piping. This allowed water in the COG condensate to freeze. The freezing blocked drains and led to the accumulation of a flammable phase in the furnace system.

2. **The Burns Harbor facility did not have a system for monitoring and controlling hazards that could be caused by changes in COG condensate flammability or accumulation rates.**

- Changes in the amount of condensate being collected were not taken into account by management. By not examining or responding to these changes, the facility missed opportunities to take corrective action, which could have prevented the February 2 incident.

- Employees were not generally aware of the potential flammability of COG condensate under certain operating conditions.

## ES. 5  Contributing Cause

**The Burns Harbor facility did not have a program to identify and address hazards that might be created by decommissioning and demolition operations.**

- The hazards created by the deadleg were not considered when the #4 furnace was decommissioned in 1992. The deadleg was not removed or protected from freezing at that time or when demolition activities began in 2000.

- The demolition work resulted in the creation of hazards, such as lack of railings on the elevated platform and obstructed egress.

## ES.6     Recommendations

### Bethlehem Steel Corporation, Burns Harbor Mill

1. Implement a work authorization program that requires higher levels of management review, approval, and oversight for jobs that present higher levels of risk, such as opening lines potentially containing flammable liquids where there is no low point drain.

2. Monitor the accumulation and flammability of COG condensate throughout the mill. Address potentially hazardous changes in condensate accumulation rates and flammability.

3. Survey the mill for deadlegs and implement a program for resolving the hazards. Develop guidance for plant personnel on the risks of deadlegs and their prevention. Include deadlegs in plant winterization planning.

4. Provide drains at low points in piping to allow for the safe draining of potentially flammable material.

5. Ensure that Burns Harbor and contractor employees are trained with regard to the potential presence of flammable liquids when working with or opening COG or condensate piping and equipment.

6.  Establish procedures to ensure that insulation is replaced when removed for maintenance.

**Bethlehem Steel Corporation**

1.  Conduct periodic audits of work authorization, line and equipment opening, deadleg management programs, and decommissioning and demolition activities at your steelmaking facilities. Share findings with the workforce.

2.  Revise the Material Safety Data Sheet (MSDS) for COG condensate to highlight the potential flammability hazard. Ensure that management at your steelmaking facilities trains employees and informs contractors with regard to the potential presence of flammable liquids when working with or opening COG condensate piping and equipment.

3.  Communicate findings of this report to the workforce and contractors at Bethlehem Steel's steelmaking facilities.

**American Iron and Steel Institute, Association of Iron and Steel Engineers, United Steelworkers of America, AFL-CIO Building Trades Council**

Communicate findings of this report to your membership.

# 1.0 INTRODUCTION

## 1.1 Background

On February 2, 2001, a fire in the furnace area of the 160-inch plate mill at Bethlehem Steel Corporation's Burns Harbor mill in Chesterton, Indiana, killed a Bethlehem Steel millwright and a supervisor with Onyx Industrial Services, a vacuum truck contractor. Another millwright was seriously injured, and three millwrights received lesser injuries. Workers were attempting to remove a slip blind[5] and a cracked valve from a coke oven gas (COG) line when flammable liquid was released and ignited.

## 1.2 Investigative Process

The U.S. Chemical Safety and Hazard Investigation Board (CSB) examined physical evidence at the site, conducted interviews, and reviewed relevant documents. The CSB incident investigation team coordinated activities with the Indiana Occupational Safety and Health Administration (IOSHA), which also investigated the incident.

CSB contracted with Phoenix Chemical Laboratory Inc. for analysis of condensate samples and with Engineering Systems Inc. for inspection of an infrared heat lamp found at the incident scene.

## 1.3 Burns Harbor Mill

The Burns Harbor mill of Bethlehem Steel is located on the shore of Lake Michigan. Burns Harbor opened in 1962. The mill, which covers approximately 3 square miles, employs about 5,000 members of the United Steelworkers of America union and 1,100 salaried personnel. There is a daily contractor population of 200 to 300.

---

[5] A slip blind (referred to as a pancake blind at Burns Harbor) is a round metal plate that is slipped between the loosened flanges of a piping connection to prevent flow.

As an integrated mill, Burns Harbor uses iron ore and coke to produce iron, which is converted to steel in three basic oxygen furnaces. Coke is produced onsite from coal in two coke oven production units.

Molten steel is converted to slabs in continuous casters. The slabs, resembling king-size mattresses in shape and weighing up to 20 tons each, are further processed into various shapes in the hot strip mill or the 160-inch plate mill, where the February 2 incident occurred.

## 1.4    160-Inch Plate Mill

The 160-inch plate mill contains two continuous and four batch furnaces (Figure 1), where steel slabs are heated to greater than 2,300 degrees Fahrenheit ($^{\circ}$F). The slabs are further processed by being passed through heavy rolls, becoming thinner and longer, until a final steel plate is produced. Either coke oven gas or natural gas is burned to heat the batch furnaces. Figure 2 shows one of the batch furnaces in operation.

## 1.5    Coke Oven Gas

Coal is carbonized to coke by heating it to a high temperature (2,200$^{\circ}$F) in an oxygen-deficient atmosphere.

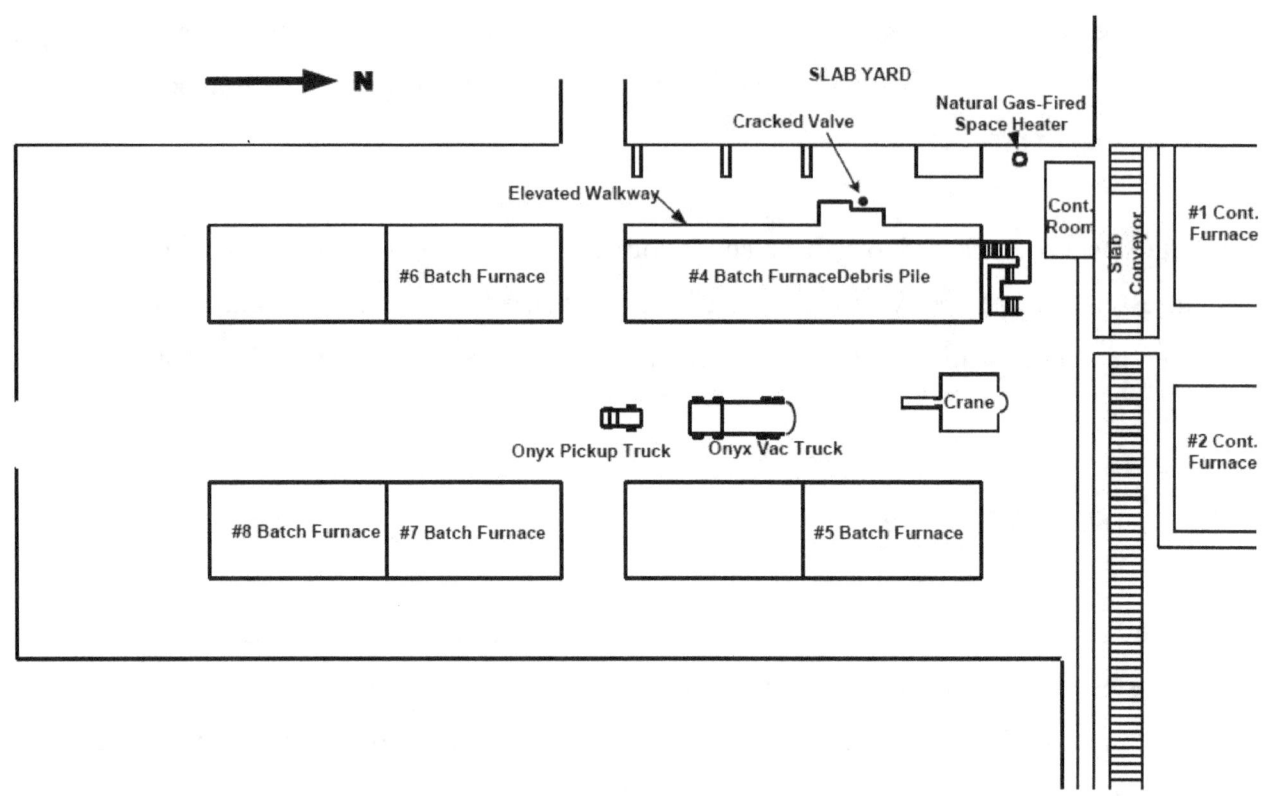

**Figure 1. Two continuous and four batch furnaces at 160-inch plate mill.**

**Figure 2. Active batch furnace showing crane removing steel slab.**

Volatile materials and gases formed in the cokemaking process are vaporized and removed, leaving the solid coke behind. At Burns Harbor, the coal chemical unit cleans the raw coke oven gas to produce fuel for use in the mill. The following steps are required to process coke oven gas:

- Cool the gas by direct contact with a liquid condensate stream, which removes the majority of the water and hydrocarbon liquids.
- Remove tar particles by electrostatic precipitation.
- Absorb ammonia in a sulfuric acid solution and convert to ammonium sulfate, a commercial byproduct.
- Remove naphthalene via direct contact washing.

Forty percent of the gas is used to heat the coke oven units, leaving 60 percent available to the rest of the mill. The COG flow rate is approximately 80 million cubic feet per day ($ft^3$/day). Gas users in the mill include a power generating station and blast furnaces. The remaining gas then continues to the hot strip mill and, finally, to the 160-inch plate mill. Excess gas not consumed by the plant is burned in a flare tower. The COG distribution system runs for several miles within the Burns Harbor facility (Figure 3).

The coal chemical unit does not remove all of the condensate from the coke oven gas. The gas enters the distribution system at a temperature of 85 to 110° F, and vapors continue to condense as the gas cools in the piping. The liquid formed is carried downstream to a series of drains located at intervals along the COG system (Figure 4), where it is collected in tanks for recycle and disposal.

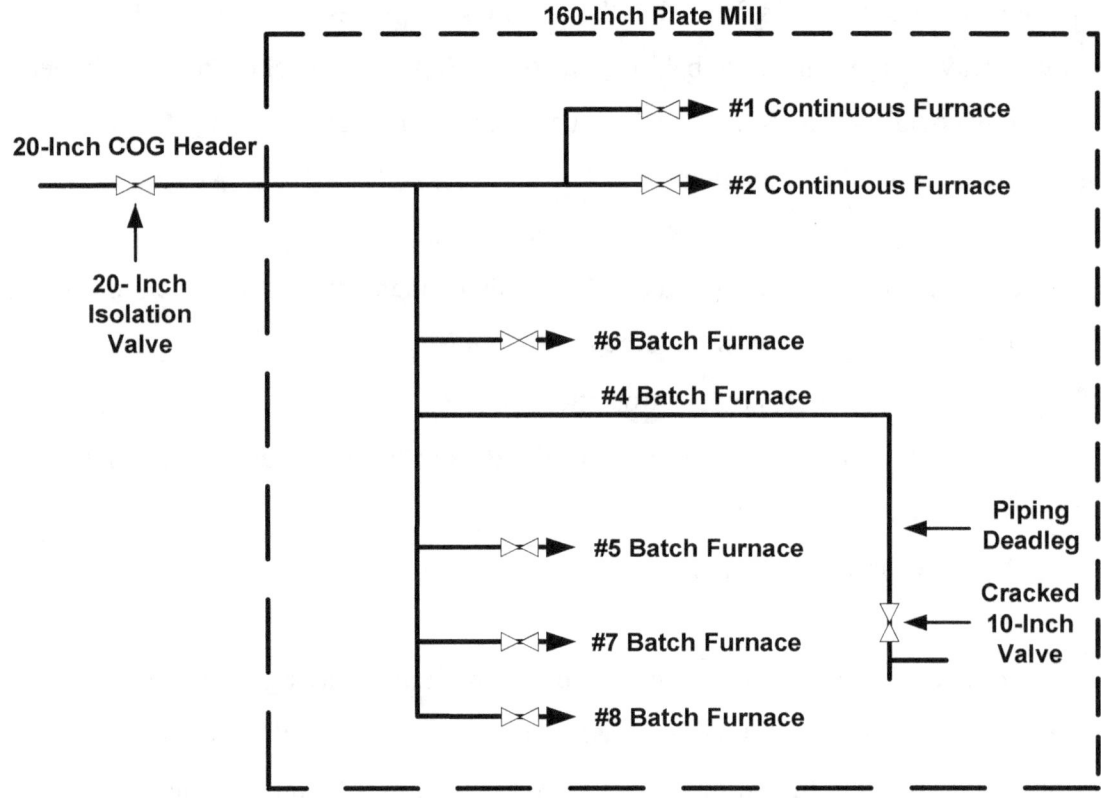

**Figure 3. COG system in 160-inch plate mill.**

The Bethlehem Steel Material Safety Data Sheet (MSDS) for coke oven gas provides the following composition data:

| Composition of Coke Oven Gas at 100°F | |
|---|---|
| Component | Weight Percent |
| Water | Approx. 10 |
| Benzene | 1 – 4 |
| Carbon monoxide | 13 – 16 |
| Carbon dioxide | 6 – 8 |
| Ethylene | 5 – 11 |
| Hydrogen | 9 – 13 |
| Methane | 43 – 53 |
| Ethane | 2 - 3 |
| Hydrogen sulfide | 0.9 – 1.5 |

The MSDS also identifies trace components, including butylenes (< 0.8 percent), toluene (< 0.5 percent), and xylenes (< 0.3 percent).[6]

The Burns Harbor MSDS for COG condensate lists a specific gravity of 1 and a boiling point of 212°F, which indicates that normally the condensate is mostly water.[7]

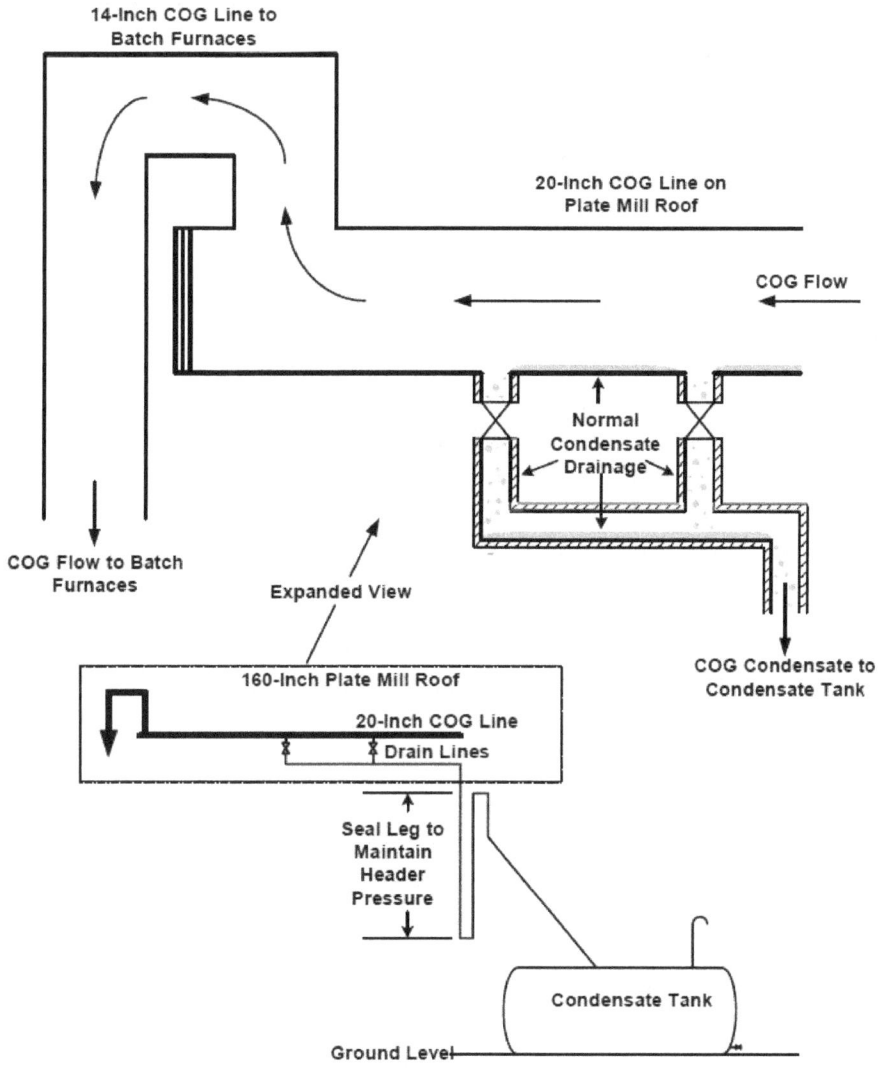

**Figure 4. Condensate removal, normal operation.**

---

[6] Bethlehem Steel Corporation, Coke Oven Gas Material Safety Data Sheet, January 1997.
[7] Bethlehem Steel Corporation, Coke Oven Gas Condensate Material Safety Data Sheet, April 1997.

## 2.0     DESCRIPTION OF INCIDENT

### 2.1     Pre-Incident Events

### 2.1.1     Furnace Decommissioning and Demolition

The #4 batch furnace in the 160-inch plate mill was shut down in 1992, at which time a 10-inch isolation gate valve was closed to prevent the flow of coke oven gas to the furnace. This created a 25-foot vertical deadleg[8] of 10-inch-diameter piping above the valve, which was open to the COG distribution piping (Figure 5). Furnace demolition began in summer 2000.

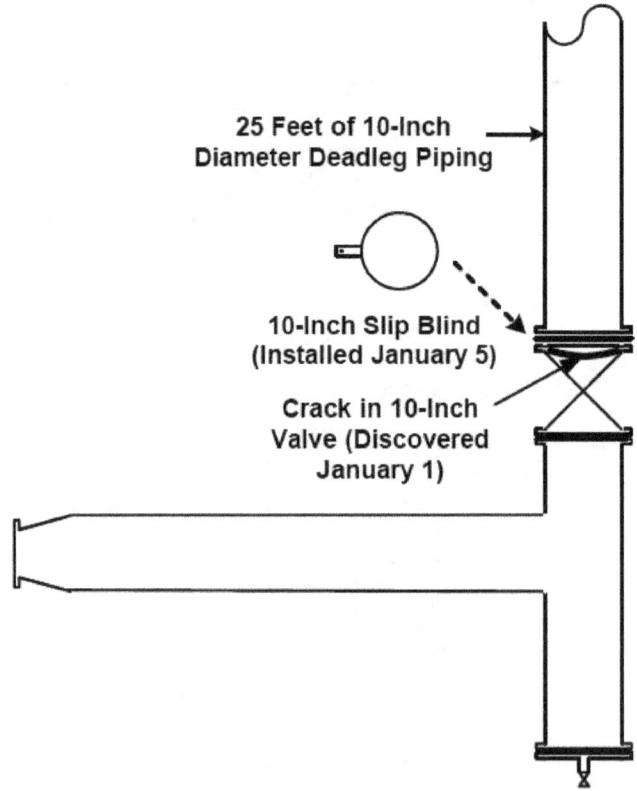

**Figure 5.   #4 Batch furnace COG piping.**

---

[8]A deadleg is a section of piping, typically vertical, without flow. In this case, it was connected to the main COG piping.

18

Over the Thanksgiving 2000 weekend, the furnace structure was knocked down. Figure 6 shows the resulting rubble pile.

**Figure 6. #4 Batch furnace debris pile present before incident.**

## 2.1.2    Discovery of Leak, January 1, 2001

On January 1, 2001, around noon, a foreman at the 160-inch plate mill detected a COG odor in the furnace area. Upon investigating, he determined that gas was leaking from a large crack in the 10-inch gate valve at the #4 furnace. The foreman contacted the utility department, which is responsible for the COG distribution system at Burns Harbor. By 4:00 pm, the main 20-inch manual gate valve located on the roof of the plate mill was closed, which stopped the flow of coke oven gas to the building. The fuel for the furnaces was switched from coke oven gas to natural gas.

CSB determined that the 10-inch valve likely cracked when water trapped in the deadleg above the valve froze and expanded. The leak became apparent as the ice thawed. Although outdoor temperatures remained below freezing for most of December, a significant warmup in the month allowed for thawing inside the furnace area. It is probable that any liquid in the deadleg drained through the crack before the gas was detected. As shown in Figure 5, the crack was located at the upper flange of the valve, above the gate that blocked flow.

### 2.1.3   Installation of Slip Blind, January 5, 2001

Before the plate mill foreman left work on January 1, he discussed the proposed repairs with a foreman from the general services department. (This department is a plant-wide group of approximately 85 employees who supplement maintenance activities in each operating area.) They determined that the best approach was to remove the cracked 10-inch valve and replace it with a blind flange fitted with a 1-inch drain valve,[9] which would serve as the drainage point for the 25-foot deadleg.

To safely proceed with the job, the foremen agreed that a purge procedure was required. At Burns Harbor, a purge procedure is a set of written instructions for preparing a line for maintenance. Purge procedures are typically written by combustion technicians,[10] in consultation with operations and safety personnel, as necessary. The purge procedure lists the order for opening and closing specific valves and vents (lockout/tagout) to ensure that hazardous gases and liquids are vented and drained prior to beginning maintenance work.

The leaking valve problem was the subject of a meeting of supervisors from the plate mill and the utility departments between January 2 and 5. The managers decided to install a slip blind in the flange above the leaking valve (Figure 5) instead of the preferred blind flange and drain valve assembly. It would have taken additional time to fabricate the blind flange and drain valve, and the plant wanted to switch more quickly from natural gas to the less expensive coke oven gas.

---

[9] A blind flange is a solid plate piping component used to close the open end of a pipe.
[10] Combustion technicians are responsible for instrumentation and for the equipment that controls and monitors the fuel gases used at Burns Harbor.

On January 5, managers and staff from the 160-inch plate mill and the utility and general services departments met on the elevated walkway at the valve to discuss installation of the slip blind. Three millwrights from the general services department were assigned to the job. They were informed that the main 20-inch COG valve was closed and that coke oven gas had been vented from the plate mill system piping. The isolation and venting were done without written pre-job planning, which is required by Burns Harbor maintenance procedures when hazardous gas might be present.

The millwrights began the work by removing two bolts and checking the flange area for flammable gases with a combustible gas detector. No hazardous gases were detected. They then proceeded with the slip blind installation. As they loosened and removed the remaining bolts, a tar-like residue with a molasses consistency began to ooze from the flange, hindering installation of the blind. The millwrights hammered the blind into the flange opening, and then reinstalled and tightened the bolts.

At some time during the following week, a foreman placed a 250-watt infrared heat lamp near the line, just above the 10-inch valve. The lamp was intended to keep the line warm, prevent freezing, and thus prevent failure of the piping and the release of additional material. Heat lamps are one of the devices commonly used at the Burns Harbor facility to prevent lines from freezing.

## 2.2    The Incident

On the morning of February 2, 2001, another meeting of management and staff from the utility and plate mill departments was held at the cracked 10-inch valve to plan the valve removal job. Personnel discussed the need to drain the line above the blind, but this could not be done safely with the blind installed. However, they decided to proceed because they believed that the condensate was nonflammable. Two potential ignition sources were located in the area when the job began–a natural gas-fired space heater and the infrared heat lamp.

The job was assigned to five general services department millwrights, including two who had originally installed the slip blind on January 5. Burns Harbor management also assigned a four-man crew from Onyx Industrial Services to capture COG condensate that might be released when the line was opened. The crew consisted of two supervisors and two vacuum truck operators.

At this time, the workers were located as shown in Figure 7. Two millwrights were balanced on the piping behind the valve, off the walkway. Another millwright was standing on the walkway. The Onyx supervisor was standing to the side of the valve. The fourth millwright was working near the end of the walkway, and the fifth millwright and three of the Onyx personnel were located on the ground.

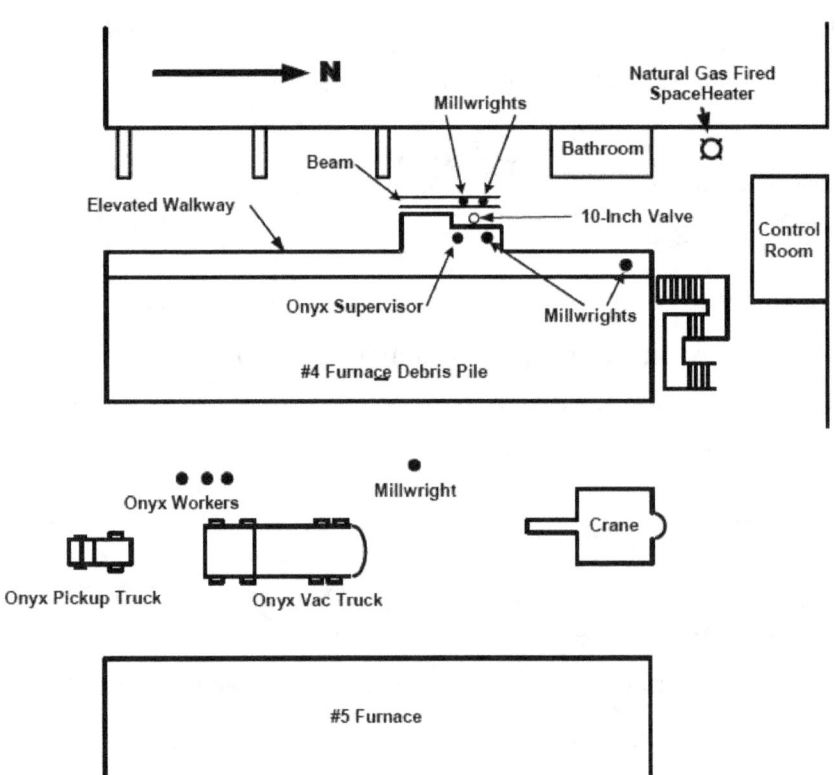

**Figure 7. Location of personnel at time of release, February 2, 2001.**

To begin the work, the millwrights removed the bolts on the bottom side of the valve, which opened up about 6 inches of space below the valve. They then loosened the bolts on the top flange of the valve, around the slip blind. A small stream of liquid began to seep from the flange, in addition to black tar-like material; and the valve suddenly dropped down several inches against the loosened bolts (Figure 8). Flammable condensate sprayed out and soaked the two millwrights positioned on the piping and the Onyx supervisor. The condensate ignited. Another millwright observed the flame move from the north and below him along the wall to the south, toward the valve. As the flame reached the valve and the now open pipe, there was a blast and flammable liquid sprayed in all directions.

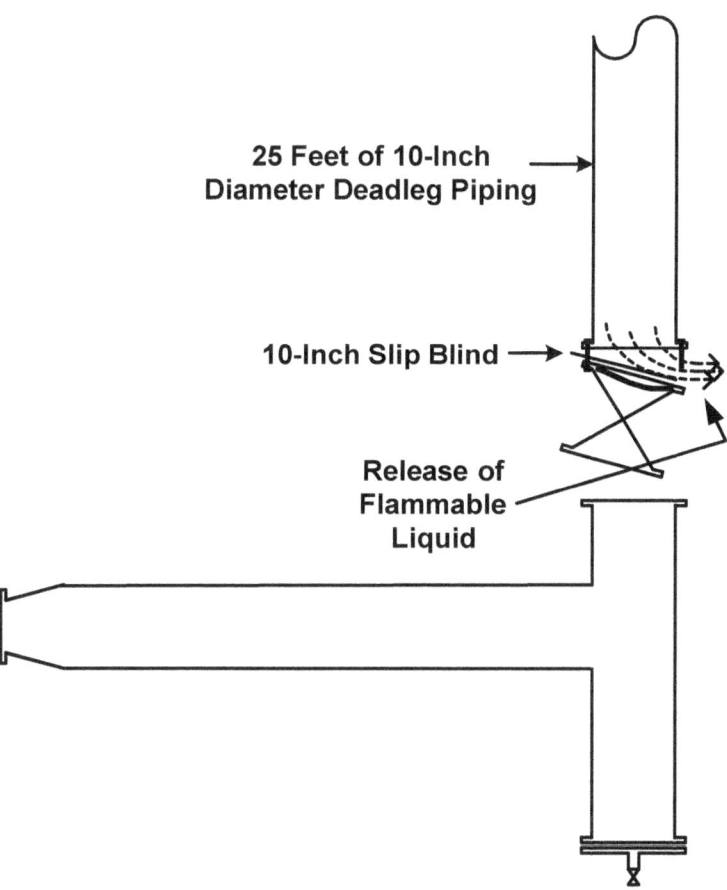

**Figure 8. #4 Batch furnace COG piping, release of flammable liquid,**

**February 2, 2001.**

The two millwrights on the piping were engulfed in the flames and fell behind the furnace structure. One of these millwrights died; the other was injured, with burns and contusions. The Onyx supervisor fell off of the east side of the walkway onto the furnace debris pile and suffered fatal burns. (There was no railing on the east side of the walkway due to the demolition activities.). The third millwright ran down through the flames across the debris pile and was seriously burned. The fourth millwright suffered smoke inhalation as he ran down the stairs through the flames.

## 3.0    ANALYSIS OF INCIDENT

CSB identified four major problem areas in the Burns Harbor 160-inch plate mill that contributed to the February 2 incident:

- Lack of understanding of the condensate's potential flammability
- Maintenance job planning and execution
- Condensate composition and removal
- Hazard communication and training.

### 3.1    Condensate Incidents in 160-Inch Plate Mill

Between the time of the initial leak on January 1 and the fire on February 2, three incidents demonstrated that the amount of condensate in the COG system was unusually high and that the liquid was not the typical nonflammable composition the workforce had come to expect.   Management did not recognize the relationship between these condensate problems and the hazards presented by repair of the cracked valve.

### 3.1.1    Fuel Switchover Problems at #5 Furnace, January 5, 2001

During the evening shift on January 5, after the slip blind was installed, the operators reopened the main 20-inch COG valve to switch the furnaces from natural gas back to coke oven gas.  After successfully switching the #1 and #2 continuous furnaces and the #7 batch furnace, the operators made the following entry into their shift log sheet: "Attempted (twice) to switch #5 furnace over to coke gas, but each time it would not light and spewed heavy black smoke – filling the mill aisle.  Because headers are apparently filled with water, it was switched back over to natural gas." This was the first indication of condensate buildup in the COG piping to the furnaces.

### 3.1.2 Fire at #2 Furnace, January 30, 2001

On January 30, flammable COG condensate reached the burners at the #2 continuous furnace (located to the north of the demolished #4 furnace), causing a large surge of fire that escaped from the doors of the furnace. Burning liquid was also observed spewing from the furnace, and the flames engulfed a walkway. Although Burns Harbor employees were in the area of the furnace, no one was injured.

In investigating the January 30 incident, Burns Harbor staff determined–prior to February 2–that condensate was not draining to the plate mill's condensate tank. A section of the condensate drain lines on the roof of the mill had likely frozen; temperatures had been below freezing, and approximately 15 feet of insulation was missing from the lines. (The missing insulation was not discovered until January 31.) Because of these conditions, the COG piping was likely full of ice, water, and flammable liquid. These conditions were not communicated by management to the personnel responsible for the planned deadleg repairs.

### 3.1.3 Condensate Leakage at #1 Furnace, January 31, 2001

On January 31, millwrights were installing a blind[11] in the COG line to isolate the #1 continuous furnace for routine maintenance. About 20 gallons of condensate leaked out. The millwrights stated that they had never seen this much condensate leak when opening the flange.

The millwrights who installed the slip blind on January 5 and worked the valve removal job on February 2 were not aware that excessive amounts of condensate were present in the COG piping system.

---

[11] The isolation blinds on the COG lines to the furnaces were "spectacle blinds," which can be pivoted in a flange. One side of the blank is open, allowing full flow; the other side is solid, preventing flow. Thus, looking at the portion of the blind that is visible outside the flange allows you to determine the flow condition inside the piping.

## 3.2    Job Planning

Planning of the maintenance work on both January 5 and February 2 was inadequate, as discussed in Sections 3.2.1 through 3.2.6.

### 3.2.1    Deadleg Hazard Control

The cracked valve discovered on January 1 was located at the bottom of a 25-foot-long vertical deadleg of 10-inch-diameter piping created when the #4 furnace was shut down. The creation of a pocket where liquid could potentially, accumulate, freeze, and subsequently crack the valve  should have been addressed by removing the deadleg or by taking steps to eliminate the potential for freezing, such as external heating and insulation.

### 3.2.2    Written Purge Procedure

Before doing maintenance work that called for COG line opening, Burns Harbor required a job-specific purge procedure in accordance with the facility's Gas Hazard Control Program.  The Burns Harbor Lockout, Blue Flag, and Tag policy was also not followed. That policy states: "Job pre-planning for work that involves confined space entry, hazardous gas work, pressure vessel work, piping work, etc., should be detailed in writing to ensure that proper Lockout, Blue Flag and Tag procedures are followed." And, "Comply with Job Safety Analysis, Purge Procedure, etc., when working on steam, gas, oil, air, acid or water lines and associated equipment.  Such equipment must be neutralized, purged, disconnected, blanked and bled of any excess energy which could cause injury."

The January 5 and February 2 jobs were conducted without a written purge procedure. This decision was made by management and staff based on the mistaken assumption that the COG condensate was not flammable and thus that the condensate remaining in the

27

line posed no threat to personnel. The requirement to execute a purge procedure was sometimes waived by operations or maintenance personnel for small jobs or jobs that were considered to be nonhazardous. However, there was no formal system for determining when the requirements could be waived.

The National Safety Council recommends: "Before working on a pipeline, shut off the line, lock and tag the valves, relieve pressure from the section of the line, and drain it." (National Safety Council, 1997; p. 117) The Occupational Safety and Health Administration's (OSHA) standard for control of hazardous energy (lockout/tagout) states: "Following the application of lockout or tagout devices to energy isolating devices, all potentially hazardous stored or residual energy shall be relieved, disconnected, restrained, and otherwise rendered safe."[12] Although a Burns Harbor blue flag (a tagout device) was placed on the 20-inch valve on the roof of the plate mill, the line was not drained.

### 3.2.3    Installation of Slip Blind

After the COG distribution piping was closed on January 1, the furnaces in the 160-inch plate mill were switched over to natural gas. Management's initial plan was to remove the cracked valve and replace it with a blind flange containing a 1-inch fitting and drain valve. This would have provided a condensate drainage point. However, on January 5, management instead decided to install a slip blind into the flange above the cracked valve.

Installation of a slip blind rather than the blind flange and drain assembly allowed the mill to more quickly return the furnaces to less expensive COG service.

---

[12] 29 CFR 1910.147 (d)(5)(i), Control of Hazardous Energy (Lockout/Tagout).

However, the slip blind eliminated the possibility of safely draining liquid that might accumulate in the deadleg.[13] Installation of the blind flange and drain valve would have provided a way to safely drain the deadleg. The United Kingdom's Health and Safety Executive (HSE) states in its book, *The Safe Isolation of Plants and Equipment*: "Bleeds and vents allow the safe depressurization of parts of the plant when it has been isolated and also enable the integrity of isolations to be checked. Inadequate provision of bleeds or vents may compromise the safety of the isolation." (HSE, 1997; p. 47)

Managers from the utility and plate mill departments recognized the risk of another line failure if the deadleg refilled with liquid and refroze. Therefore, they scheduled the installation of the blind flange and drain assembly for February 2. As an interim measure to prevent the deadleg from refreezing, an infrared heat lamp was placed next to the 10-inch piping, just above the blind.

### 3.2.4    Ignition Sources

There were two potential ignition sources in the area when the job began, though CSB could not determine which source ignited the fire:

- A natural gas-fired space heater was located 28 feet horizontally and 18 feet below the 10-inch valve. These heaters were used as part of the Burns Harbor freeze protection program for piping containing water.

---

[13] Burns Harbor personnel briefly considered, but ultimately rejected, the use of a hot tap to drain the deadleg above the slip blind. Hot tapping is a technique for creating an opening in piping that is in service by welding a fitting onto the pipe and then cutting or drilling a hole through the welded fitting. Hot tapping is normally done only when there is sufficient flow in the piping to safely dissipate heat or a sufficient amount of liquid above the weld point, and when it can be ensured that the piping does not contain a flammable atmosphere. The line above the dead leg had no flow through it, and there was no way to ascertain that the contents of the pipe would not ignite.

- An infrared heat lamp was positioned next to the 10-inch piping, above the cracked valve. CSB determined that the lamp was on at the time of the release.

Because the work involved opening a line that potentially contained flammables, job planning should have included removal of potential ignition sources. Although the Burns Harbor Gas Hazard Control Program required that representatives from the fire and safety departments assist in job planning, no one from either department was consulted in preparing for the maintenance work.

### 3.2.5    Hazards Created by Demolition Activity

The #4 furnace was shut down in 1992. In summer 2000, mill management decided to remove the furnace structure. No procedure was written for demolition of the furnace, and no safety review was conducted to consider the possible hazards created by the demolition activities.

Over the Thanksgiving 2000 weekend, the mill's crane was used to knock down the furnace. Figure 6 shows the resulting rubble pile (for comparison, see the photo of an operating furnace in Figure 2).

As a result of this destruction, the working area around the cracked valve was hazardous. The following problems were present on February 2, 2001:
- No railing was in place on the east side of the walkway; there was a 6-foot drop from the walkway to the rubble pile (Figure 9).
- Piping from the demolition blocked the stairway landing to the walkway.
- The stairway did not connect with the walkway.

These obstructions and lack of handrails made it difficult for workers to escape the area when the leak and fire started. It is probable that the loss of life and injuries would have been lessened if an easier means of exit was available. The job planning process should have addressed exit routes.

**Figure 9. Elevated walkway looking south (note absence of handrail on left side).**

### 3.2.6   Communication of Safety and Maintenance Procedures

Safety information was ineffectively transferred from management to the millwrights and contractors performing the maintenance work. All communication between the plate mill and millwright supervisors and between the supervisors and the millwrights and contractors was verbal. The millwrights and Onyx personnel stated that neither on January 5 nor February 2 were they informed of any flammables that might be present or of the previous incidents.

As explained by the National Safety Council and OSHA, good practice includes the use of safety permits to spell out the safety requirements of maintenance jobs. Safety permits are developed by supervision or authorized individuals and provide details on how a job is to be done, what hazards are involved, and any other special safety considerations. The permits are then reviewed with maintenance workers at the job site to ensure that they understand the scope and hazards of each job. The millwrights performing the work on January 5 and February 2 received no written instructions.

Had safety permits been written for the jobs, it is likely that the lack of a drain would have been identified. This would have prompted personnel to look at alternative ways to set up the work and would likely have prevented the incident or lessened its severity.

The process of preparing and following a safety work permit or a purge procedure would also have given Burns Harbor staff an opportunity to take other safety measures that might have prevented the incident or mitigated its consequences, such as removing sources of ignition, improving egress from the work area, or providing a fire watch with a charged fire hose.

## 3.3    Condensate Composition and Removal

### 3.3.1    Deadleg

When the #4 furnace was shut down in 1992, the 10-inch COG isolation valve leading to the furnace was closed, which created a 25-foot-long deadleg of vertical piping above the valve. As explained in Section 2.1.1, a deadleg is a section of piping, typically vertical, without flow. In a COG piping system, liquids may collect in deadlegs.

CSB determined that the 10-inch valve probably cracked due to the freezing and expansion of water. The crack was located at the upper flange of the valve, above the valve gate that blocked flow. After the slip blind was installed on January 5, the deadleg was still present and provided a site for COG condensate to continue to accumulate.

### 3.3.2  Presence of Flammable Liquids in COG Piping

The coke oven gas leaving the coal chemical unit, at an average temperature of 100°F, typically contained 10 percent water vapor.  As the gas stream passed through the COG distribution system and the temperature dropped, the water and heavier hydrocarbons (including benzene, toluene, and xylenes) condensed out of the gas.   The condensate drained from the bottom of the piping and into tanks located along the piping route.  Vacuum trucks periodically emptied the tanks.  Figure 3 depicts the normal operation of condensate drains on the COG line.

In August 1999, millwrights removed insulation from the COG condensate drain lines, located on the roof of the plate mill, to perform maintenance.  The insulation was not replaced.   The winterization program for the plate mill consisted of a checklist of preventive measures for locations known to be susceptible to freezing, but it did not call for a survey or inspection to identify other areas that might require or might have lost freeze protection.

The ambient temperature at the Burns Harbor mill between mid-December and mid-January was generally below freezing.  Around the middle of December 2000, the COG condensate stopped draining to the tank at the plate mill.  Without pipeline insulation, the water in the condensate probably froze, plugging the drain lines.   It is likely that water then began to build up and freeze in the COG distribution piping.   As the water froze, flammable material remained in the liquid state and floated on top of the water and ice (Figure 10).

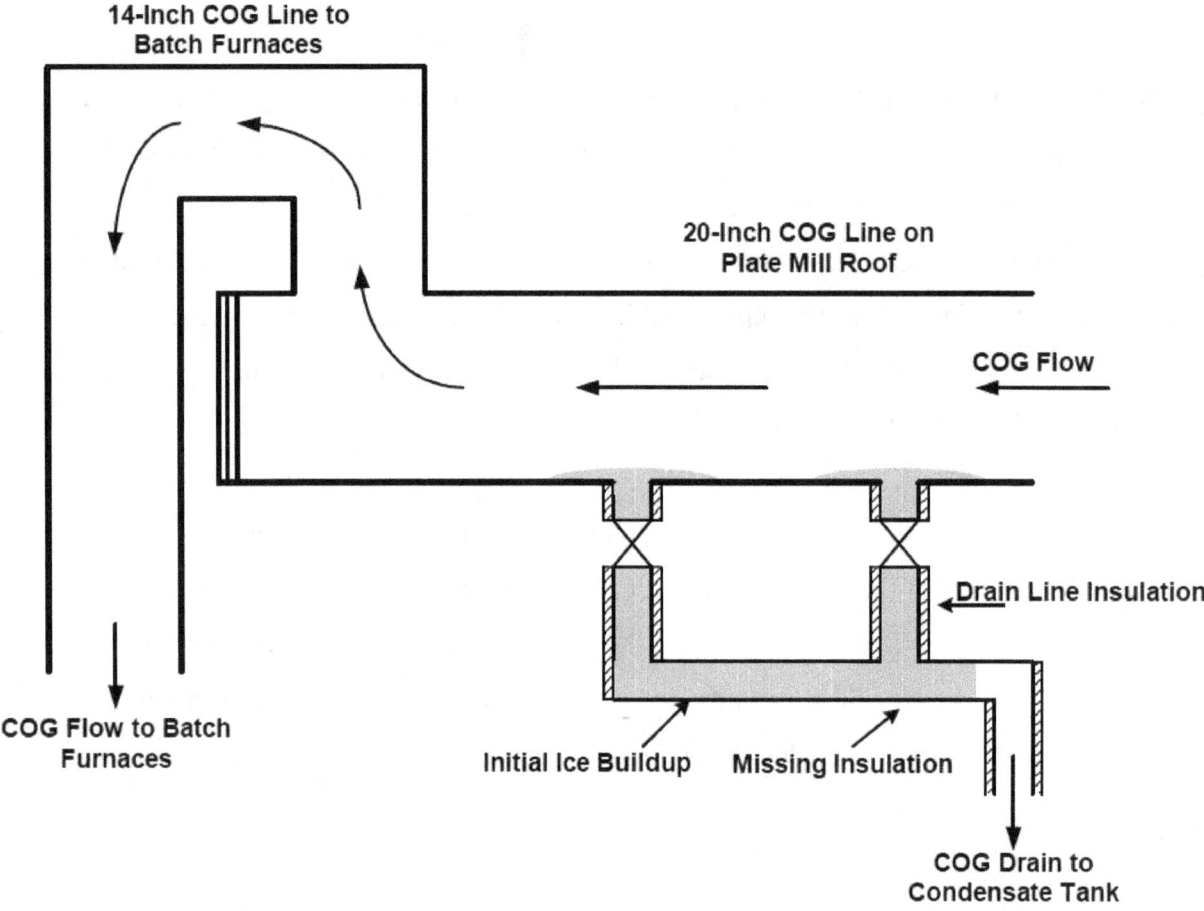

**14-Inch COG Line to Batch Furnaces**

**20-Inch COG Line on Plate Mill Roof**

**COG Flow**

**COG Flow to Batch Furnaces**

**Drain Line Insulation**

**Initial Ice Buildup**   **Missing Insulation**

**COG Drain to Condensate Tank**

**Figure 10.  Probable flammable liquid buildup scenario-ice formation.**

As the liquid/ice level in the COG piping increased, it is likely that the flammable liquid phase either flowed over the top of it or was entrained with the coke oven gas into the furnace lines (Figure 11).  This flammable liquid carryover probably settled in the lowest points of the piping, such as the deadleg at the #4 furnace–from which it was subsequently released and ignited.

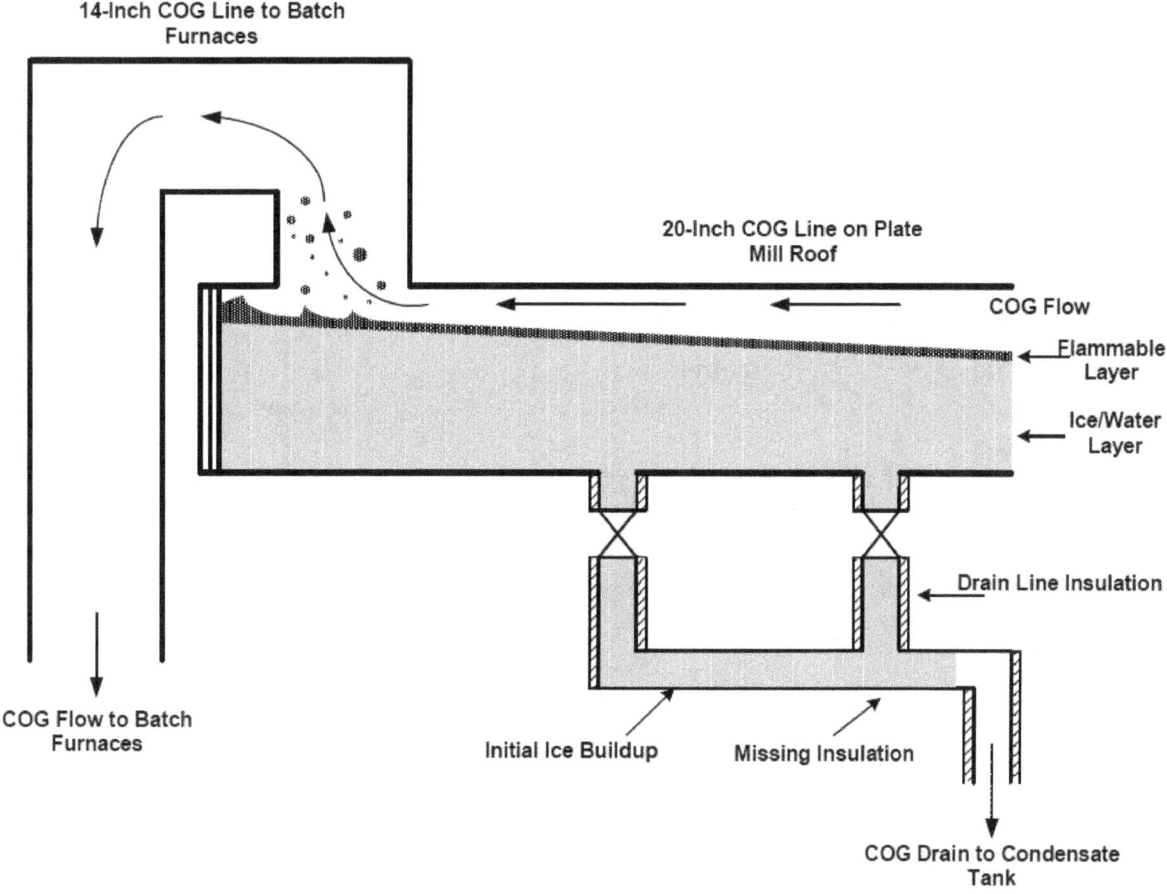

**Figure 11. Probable flammable liquid carryover scenario.**

There was a previous incident at Burns Harbor of ice buildup in COG condensate lines. In January 1997, a 72-inch-diameter overhead COG line to the blast furnace failed and fell to the ground due to the weight of ice in the piping; there was no ignition.

On February 14, 2001, CSB obtained a sample of liquid from the condensate drain at the #5 batch furnace. Because this drain was last emptied in early January, the sample was probably similar in composition to the material that was released from the deadleg at the #4 furnace and ignited on February 2. The sample had a flash point of 29°F.[14, 15]

---

[14] Flash point is the minimum temperature at which a liquid gives off sufficient vapor to form an ignitable mixture with air near the surface.

[15] The sample contained 22.4 percent benzene, 16.8 percent toluene, 13.7 percent xylenes, and 0.08 percent water. The specific gravity of the mixture was 0.92. The balance of the sample consisted of heavier organics, mostly tars.

### 3.3.3   Change in Condensate Removal Rate

Onyx Industrial Services used vacuum trucks to empty the COG condensate tanks. On a weekly basis, Onyx supplied the utility department with a printed summary of the amount of condensate withdrawn from each tank each day. However, neither the tanks nor the vacuum trucks were equipped with level or flow gauges to measure the amount of material transferred. If no condensate was withdrawn from a tank, the Onyx daily summary indicated a zero for that vessel.

The condensate tanks were normally emptied several times per week. No condensate was withdrawn from the plate mill tank from December 11, 2000, until the end of January 2001. However, during the same period, twice the normal amount of condensate was withdrawn from a condensate tank located along the COG distribution piping upstream of the plate mill's tank– indicating that condensate was backing up in the piping behind the ice buildup. No actions were taken to investigate or correct the problem.

Changes in operating parameters, such as condensate removal rates, should be analyzed to determine if they might have a significant effect on safety. Management should compare such data to a previously defined acceptable range and investigate deviations. By not having accurate data and by not responding to the information that was available, Burns Harbor missed an opportunity to take corrective action, which could have prevented the incident on February 2.

### 3.4   Hazard Communication and Training

The majority of the Bethlehem Steel employees interviewed by CSB did not believe that COG condensate presented a flammability hazard. Of 11 Burns Harbor supervisors interviewed by CSB, only four considered COG condensate to be potentially flammable and one did not know. Eight of 18 hourly employees considered it to be potentially flammable, and seven did not know. Most of the Onyx Industrial Services personnel interviewed also considered COG condensate to be mostly water. Workers familiar with the coal chemical area were aware of the potential flammability of the condensate.

Bethlehem Steel employees attended OSHA-required hazard communication training, which covered the flammability of coke oven gas and the fact that it contained a large amount of carbon monoxide. However, there was no discussion of the potential flammability hazards of the condensate.

The Bethlehem Steel MSDS for COG condensate does not mention flammability as a hazard. It was considered to be normally nonflammable. However, the liquid in the #4 furnace on February 2 was flammable because of the separation of water and flammable hydrocarbons into layers (as described in Section 3.3.2).

## 4.0  ROOT AND CONTRIBUTING CAUSES

### 4.1  Root Causes

1. **Management systems for the supervision, planning, and execution of maintenance work were inadequate.**

   - Burns Harbor mill personnel often bypassed the Lockout, Blue Flag, and Tag and Gas Hazard Control Program procedures when performing COG line maintenance in the steel handling areas of the facility. Company requirements for written planning, job setup, and line isolation and purging were not followed on January 5 or February 2.

   - The work on January 5 and February 2 should not have been scheduled without a plan to control the hazards created by the potential for flammables and by the lack of a low point drain in the deadleg.

   - Personnel performing the work were not made aware of the possible presence of flammables, nor were they informed of the condensate incidents that occurred prior to February 2.

   - Obstructed exit routes due to demolition work on the #4 furnace were not considered during job planning.

   - Insulation was not reinstalled after the completion of maintenance work on an outdoor section of system piping. This allowed water in the COG condensate to freeze. The freezing blocked drains and led to the accumulation of a flammable phase in the furnace system.

2. **The Burns Harbor facility did not have a system for monitoring and controlling hazards that could be caused by changes in COG condensate flammability or accumulation rates.**

   - Changes in the amount of condensate being collected were not taken into account by management. By not examining or responding to these changes, the facility missed opportunities to take corrective action, which could have prevented the February 2 incident.

- Employees were not generally aware of the potential flammability of COG condensate under certain operating conditions.

## 4.2 Contributing Cause

**The Burns Harbor facility did not have a program to identify and address hazards that might be created by decommissioning and demolition operations.**

- The hazards created by the deadleg were not considered when the #4 furnace was decommissioned in 1992. The deadleg was not removed or protected from freezing at that time or when demolition activities began in 2000.
- The demolition work resulted in the creation of hazards, such as lack of railings on the elevated platform and obstructed egress.

## 5.0    RECOMMENDATIONS

**Bethlehem Steel Corporation, Burns Harbor Mill**

1.  Implement a work authorization program that requires higher levels of management review, approval, and oversight for jobs that present higher levels of risk, such as opening lines potentially containing flammable liquids where there is no low point drain.  (2001-02-I-IN-R1)

2.  Monitor the accumulation and flammability of COG condensate throughout the mill.  Address potentially hazardous changes in condensate accumulation rates and flammability.  (2001-02-I-IN-R2)

3.  Survey the mill for deadlegs and implement a program for resolving the hazards. Develop guidance for plant personnel on the risks of deadlegs and their prevention.  Include deadlegs in plant winterization planning. (2001-02-I-IN-R3)

4.  Provide drains at low points in piping to allow for the safe draining of potentially flammable material.  (2001-02-I-IN-R4)

5.  Ensure that Burns Harbor and contractor employees are trained with regard to the potential presence of flammable liquids when working with or opening COG or condensate piping and equipment.  (2001-02-I-IN-R5)

6.  Establish procedures to ensure that insulation is replaced when removed for maintenance.  (2001-02-I-IN-R6)

**Bethlehem Steel Corporation**

1.  Conduct periodic audits of work authorization, line and equipment opening, deadleg management programs, and decommissioning and demolition activities at

your steelmaking facilities. Share findings with the workforce. (2001-02-I-IN-R7)

2. Revise the Material Safety Data Sheet (MSDS) for COG condensate to highlight the potential flammability hazard. Ensure that management at your steelmaking facilities trains employees and informs contractors with regard to the potential presence of flammable liquids when working with or opening COG condensate piping and equipment. (2001-02-I-IN-R8)

3. Communicate findings of this report to the workforce and contractors at Bethlehem Steel's steelmaking facilities. (2001-02-I-IN-R9)

**American Iron and Steel Institute, Association of Iron and Steel Engineers, United Steelworkers of America, AFL-CIO Building Trades Council**

Communicate findings of this report to your membership. (2001-02-I-IN-R10)

---

By the

**U.S. Chemical Safety and Hazard Investigation Board**

Gerald V. Poje, Ph.D.
Member

Isadore Rosenthal, Ph.D.
Member

Andrea Kidd Taylor, Dr. P.H.
Member

December 6, 2001

## 6.0   REFERENCES

Health and Safety Executive (HSE), 1997. *The Safe Isolation of Plants and Equipment*, Oil Industry Advisory Committee, Norwich, U.K.:  HSE Books.

National Safety Council, 1997. *Accident Prevention Manual for Business and Industry, Engineering, and Technology*, 19th Edition.

# Appendix A:  Incident Timeline

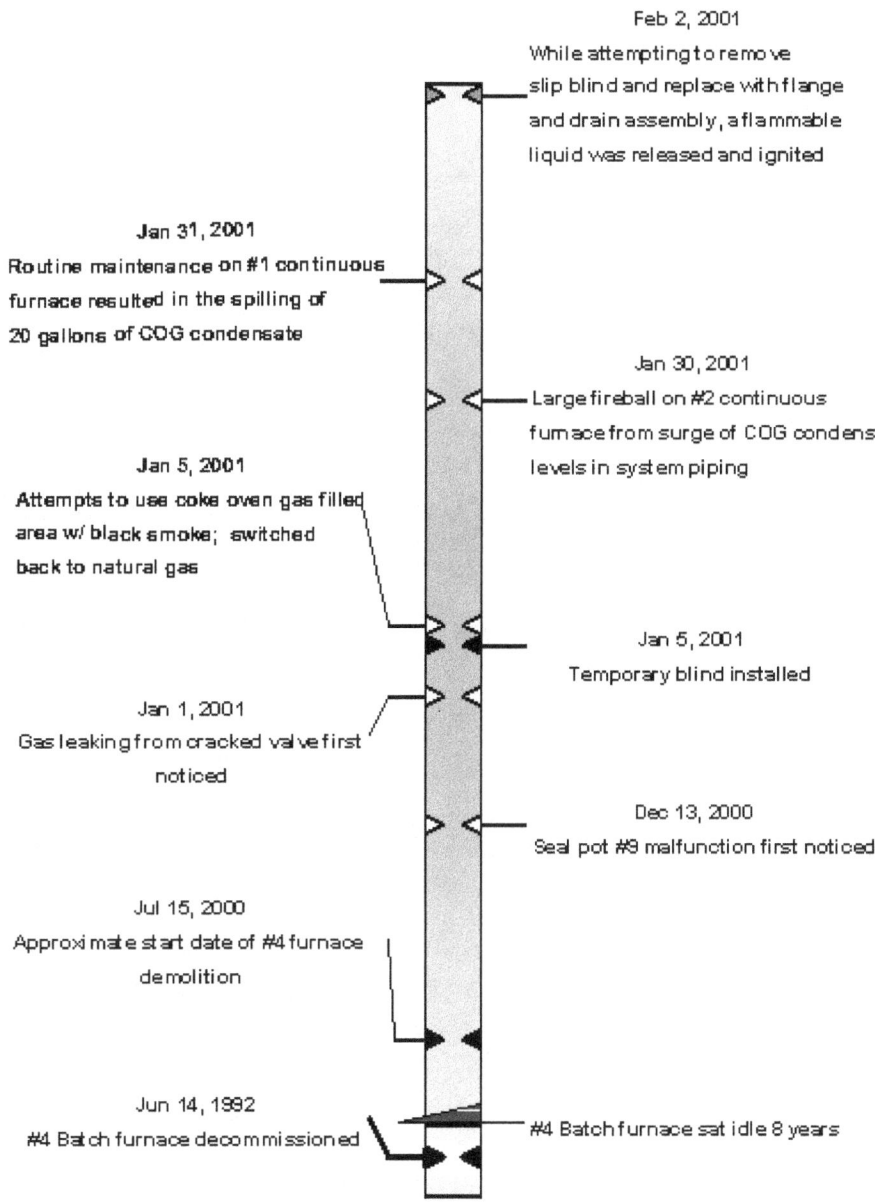

**Feb 2, 2001**
While attempting to remove slip blind and replace with flange and drain assembly, a flammable liquid was released and ignited

**Jan 31, 2001**
Routine maintenance on #1 continuous furnace resulted in the spilling of 20 gallons of COG condensate

**Jan 30, 2001**
Large fireball on #2 continuous furnace from surge of COG condens levels in system piping

**Jan 5, 2001**
Attempts to use coke oven gas filled area w/ black smoke; switched back to natural gas

**Jan 5, 2001**
Temporary blind installed

**Jan 1, 2001**
Gas leaking from cracked valve first noticed

**Dec 13, 2000**
Seal pot #9 malfunction first noticed

**Jul 15, 2000**
Approximate start date of #4 furnace demolition

**Jun 14, 1992**
#4 Batch furnace decommissioned

#4 Batch furnace sat idle 8 years

www.ingramcontent.com/pod-product-compliance
Lightning Source LLC
Chambersburg PA
CBHW081402170526
45166CB00010B/3180